ARCHITECTURE
AND
HOW TO SKETCH IT.

ILLUSTRATED BY SKETCHES OF TYPICAL EXAMPLES.

BY

H. W. ROBERTS.

Author of " R.'s Method of Perspective," " Rhythmic Designing,"
"Architectural Sketching and Drawing in Perspective."

Copyright © 2013 Read Books Ltd.
This book is copyright and may not be
reproduced or copied in any way without
the express permission of the publisher in writing

British Library Cataloguing-in-Publication Data
A catalogue record for this book is available from the
British Library

Drawing and Illustration

Drawing is a form of visual art that can make use of any number of drawing instruments, including graphite pencils, pen and ink, inked brushes, wax colour pencils, crayons, charcoal, chalk, pastels and various kinds of erasers, markers, styluses, metals (such as silverpoint) and even electronic drawing. As a medium, it has been one of the most popular and fundamental means of public expression throughout human history – as one of the simplest and most efficient means of communicating visual ideas.

Drawing itself long predates other forms of human communication, with evidence for its existence preceding that of the written word – demonstrated in cave paintings of around 40,000 years ago. These drawings, known as pictograms, depicted objects and abstract concepts including animals, human hands and generalised patterns. Over time, these sketches and paintings were stylised and simplified, leading to the development of the written language as we know it today. This form of drawing can truly be considered art in its purest sense – the basic forms on which all others build.

Whilst the term 'to draw' derives from the Old English *dragan* (meaning 'to drag, draw or protract'), the word 'illustrate' derives from the Latin word *illustratio*, meaning 'enlighten' or 'irradiate'. This process of 'enlightenment' is central to drawing and illustration as we know it today. Medieval codices' illustrations were often called 'illuminations', designed to highlight and further explain important aspects of biblical texts. This was the most general form of illustration; hand-created, individual and unique. This changed in the fifteenth century however, when books began to be illustrated with woodcuts – most notably in Germany, by Albrecht Dürer.

The first creative impulses of a painter or sculptor are commonly expressed in drawings, and architects and photographers are commonly trained to draw, if for no other reason than to train their perceptual skills and develop their creative potential. Initially, artists used and re-used wooden tablets for the production of their drawings, however following the widespread availability of paper in the fourteenth century, the use of drawing in the arts increased. During the Renaissance (a period of massive flourishing of human intellectual endeavours and creativity), drawings exhibiting realistic and representational qualities emerged. Notable draftsmen included Leonardo da Vinci, Michelangelo and Raphael. They were inspired by the concurrent developments in geometry and philosophy, exhibiting a true synthesis of these branches – a combination somewhat lost in the modern day.

Figure drawing became a recognised subsection of artistic drawing in this period, despite its long history stretching back to prehistoric descriptions. An anecdote by the Roman author and philosopher Pliny, describes how Zeuxis (a painter who flourished during the 5th century BCE) reviewed the young women of Agrigentum naked before selecting five whose features he would combine in order to paint an ideal image. The use of nude models in the medieval artist's workshop is further implied in the writings of Cennino Cennini (an Italian painter), and a manuscript of Villard de Honnecourt confirms that sketching from life was an established practice by the thirteenth century. The Carracci, who opened their *Accademia degli Incamminati* (one of the first art academies in Italy) in Bologna in the 1580s, set the pattern for later art schools by making life drawing the central discipline. The course of training began with the copying of engravings, then proceeded to drawing from plaster casts, after which the students were trained in drawing from the live model.

The main processes for reproduction of drawings and illustrations in the sixteenth and seventeenth centuries were engraving and etching, and by the end of the eighteenth century, lithography (a method of printing originally based on the immiscibility of oil and water) allowed even better illustrations to be reproduced. In the later seventeenth and eighteenth centuries, the previous combination of the arts and sciences in drawing gave way to a more romantic and even classical style, epitomised by draftsmen such as Poussin, Rembrandt, Rubens, Tiepolo and Antoine Watteau. Mastery in drawing was considered a prerequisite to painting, and students in Jacques-Louis David's Studio (a famed eighteenth century French painter of the neo-classical style), were required to draw for six hours a day, from a model who remained in the same pose for an entire week!

During this period, an increasingly large gap started to emerge between 'fine artists' on the one hand, and 'draftsmen' / 'illustrators' on the other. This difference became further complicated with the 'Golden Age of Illustration'; a period customarily defined as lasting from the latter quarter of the nineteenth century until just after the First World War. In this period of no more than fifty years the popularity, abundance and most importantly the unprecedented upsurge in quality of illustrated works marked an astounding change in the way that publishers, artists and the general public came to view artistic drawing. Arthur Rackham, Walter Crane, John Tenniel and William Blake are some of its most famous names. Until the latter part of the nineteenth century, the work of illustrators was largely proffered anonymously, and in England it was only after Thomas Bewick's pioneering technical advances in wood engraving that it became common to acknowledge the artistic and technical expertise of illustrators. Such draftsmen also frequently used their drawings in preparation for paintings, further obfuscating the distinction between drawing/painting, high/low art.

The artists involved in the Arts and Crafts Movement (with a strong emphasis on stylised drawing, and a powerful influence on the 'Golden Age of Illustration') also attempted to counter the ever intruding Industrial Revolution, by bringing the values of beautiful and inventive craftsmanship back into the sphere of everyday life. This helped to counter the main challenge which emerged around this time – photography. The invention of the first widely available form of photography (with flexible photographic film role marketed in 1885) led to a shift in the use of drawing in the arts. This new technology took over from drawing as a superior method of accurately representing the visual world, and many artists abandoned their painstaking drawing practices. As a result of these developments however, modernism in the arts emerged – encouraging 'imaginative originality' in drawing and abstract formulations. Drawing was once again at the forefront of the arts.

There are many different categories of drawing, including figure drawing, cartooning, doodling and shading. There are also many drawing methods, such as line drawing, stippling, shading, hatching, crosshatching, creating textures and tracing – and the artist must be aware of complex problems such as form, proportion and perspective (portrayed in either linear methods, or depth through tone and texture). Today, there are also many computer-aided drawing tools, which are utilised in design, architecture, engineering, as well as the fine arts. It is often exploratory, with considerable emphasis on observation, problem-solving and composition, and as such, remains an unceasingly useful tool in the artists repertoire.

The processes of drawing is a fascinating artistic practice, enabling a beautiful array of effects and creative expression. As is evident from this short introduction, it also has an incredibly old history, moving from decorations on cave walls to the most advanced, realistic and imaginative drawings possible in the present day. It is hoped that the current reader enjoys this book on the subject.

PREFACE.

THE greater qualities of Art are God-given and can be learned from no school or master; but all means of expression and processes are mechanical, and can be imparted much more quickly than some people imagine, if up-to-date methods of teaching are used, and the student has the desire and will give the attention.

As in language a limited vocabulary is sufficient for a very numerous class, so the latent power of drawing may have been but slightly developed, but that power can be considerably increased by any individual who so desires and so determines. "Nihil sine labore" is as true to-day as ever it was. The outflow of a ripe mind stored with facts accumulated by great labour, may be an impression, or the slightest sketch executed in a few minutes, and yet be priceless; while the overflow of a shallow reservoir need not be taken seriously, as it is valueless—nothing without labour—without great labour, but we have no time for needless labour such as drawing circles without compasses, straight lines and geometrical figures without instruments.

"Ars longa vita brevis," yes, Art is long and life short, but just as we try to make life longer and fuller, we must try to make Art shorter and nearer. A great deal that has been written on Art and the old slow way of teaching it, is now, compared with modern methods,

PREFACE

as much out of date as the old carrier's cart, when compared with the modern motor car. To-day we go much more quickly by using every aid the ingenuity of man can supply. The old artists prepared their own colours, their canvases and tools. To-day we 'phone or wire instructions to our Artist-colourman, and by return of post have our requirements at hand, in every case feeling sure that we get the best possible, carefully made by experts in each branch who have the command of the most up-to-date manufacturing appliances.

CONTENTS.

	PAGE
PREFACE	5
THE AIM	9
VISIT TO AN IDEAL CITY	13
WITHOUT THE WALLS	14
WITHIN THE WALLS	21
WITHOUT THE CHURCH	24
WITHIN THE CHURCH	31
METHOD IN SKETCHING TO GET RAPID AND ACCURATE REPRESENTATION . . .	44
A SIMPLE BUILDING	48
OUTSIDE OF A CHURCH	51
INSIDE OF A CHURCH	52
OCTAGONAL FORMS	53
ARCHES	54
CIRCLES ON PLAN	56

ARCHITECTURE AND HOW TO SKETCH IT.

THE AIM.

THE numerous camera-carrying visitors to our old Historical Buildings show how very general is their wish to personally record whatever may at the moment most particularly impress them.

Interesting as it may be to record by photograph, I think it is yet far more satisfactory to be able to make a convincing sketch, and with modern methods it is possible to learn to sketch rapidly and accurately, in less time than it takes to become a really good photographer. After a long experience, I can imagine no greater possible enjoyment, as one goes through life, than sketching from the endless beauties of Nature, and the numerous Art and Architectural works of the past. Surely there is no more pleasant way of getting useful information; as here—in Great Britain—we can find so much to learn from the stone-built history of our churches, and if we get into the habit of sketching as we go, we not only learn more deeply, but get an instructive and valuable series of records of our travels, interesting equally to ourselves and to all who may afterwards see them. My own collection contains: Roman Remains; The Celtic Crosses of Ireland; Saxon and Norman Work; The Gothic Work of the Early English, Decorated and Perpendicular Periods;

The Early Renaissance, as shown in the Elizabethan and Early Jacobean Periods ; The Late Renaissance ; Georgian and Modern Work. From nearly every church one can readily learn to read local history ; to decide when the various parts have been constructed, and to approximately fix dates ; in some cases going back to pre-Conquest times. In many a village church one can find architecture of three periods, with interesting Tudor, Jacobean, Georgian, and modern monuments, extending over a period of nearly 1,000 years.

For about half a century I have known and enjoyed the charm of Architectural Sketching, a pleasure in no way decreasing, and I find subjects far too numerous to be ever exhausted. From the many interesting experiences I have had, in individually helping others to get over the initiatory difficulties of starting to sketch, I now take a particular interest in endeavouring to show by written description how Architectural features may be truthfully represented, by all who desire to do so, who may not have had previous experience in drawing such subjects ; and further, while not in any way attempting, in so small a book, to go over the ground so well done by Paley, in " Manual of Gothic Architecture " ; by Parker, in " Glossary of Architecture " and " ABC of Gothic Architecture " ; by Rickman, in " Gothic Architecture " and "Attempt to Discriminate the Styles of Architecture "—the textbooks of 50 years ago ; or in modern books, such as Bond's " Gothic Architecture " ; Prior's " History of Gothic Art in England," and " Mediaeval Figure Sculpture,"—a book of 700 pages and 800 illustrations—in which the Author says he is but "a pioneer in an untrodden country," I yet hope to say enough to interest the ordinary visitors, and to point out sufficient indication of date, so that they may be able to read for themselves some of the stone-built history; that they may the better understand the many excellent local guides to the churches, and follow with more interest the generally intelligent verger who shows the individual beauties of his church. But local information is sometimes more amusing than reliable. I remember hearing a large party of visitors being told, "All this work was done by the Romans a many year ago"—it happened to be a very beautiful 14th-century Lady Chapel. One of the party then said, "Dear me, why this will be nearly 2,000 years old." The attendant, an old man not deep in figures and facts replied, "Oh yes, yes, I daresay, very old, very old." By the Romans the old man evidently meant the Roman Catholics.

I wish as far as possible to help the would-be sketcher to start working; but first, I will show some important points in Representation; how all form is modified by its position in relation to the eye level, and to its distance away from the observer; and afterwards, in a series of Diagrammatic Illustrations, endeavour to clearly indicate how the more ordinary Architectural forms actually appear, and how they must be represented in a convincing sketch. I had perhaps better explain here what I mean by a convincing sketch.

1. A good painting, beyond the higher qualities of selection, composition, etc., should show correct form, proportion, tone, colour.

2. A good etching may have the same higher qualities, correct form, and proportion, and ignore tone and colour.

3. A good photograph will probably have fewer of the higher qualities, but absolutely correct form and proportion, a modified light and shade and no colour.

Different mediums of working have their limitations, yet the results may be altogether satisfactory if they faithfully show a small part of the truth.

When working in pencil or pen and ink, the medium is very limited; it is perhaps the more necessary that the given moiety is correct. We can leave out all weak effects, and reduce our representation to a few suggestive touches, if the qualities retained are so absolutely correct that the beholders are convincingly satisfied. A convincing sketch may be the work of a few minutes and yet be absolutely correct as far as it goes.

If you have a difficulty in keeping your drawing upright, use a set square to help you keep right, or use the sketch books made with Bank Note paper, which is transparent, and put a sheet of paper with squares ruled on it underneath the sheet you sketch on.

All aids and devices that are or can be made for drawing more rapidly and accurately are extremely useful, and Art workers use every practical idea they can get in their particular craft to ensure greater accuracy and rapidity.

AND HOW TO SKETCH IT. 13

VISIT TO AN IDEAL CITY.

Before giving the truths of Architectural Representation, which are essential in any and every drawing or sketch, I beg you to accompany me on an afternoon visit to a very ideal church, particularly rich in varied examples of English Architecture, and instead of taking any actual church in one particular locality, which would entirely localise the examples, I propose to select my illustrations from sketches I have made in all parts of our country, so that the information may apply in some measure when used in any part of Great Britain.

Our knowledge of Architecture has considerably broadened since my young days, when we were taught to appreciate the Early English work of the 13th century, to just countenance the 14th and 15th century, and to condemn all post - Reformation Architecture. The wonderful work of Sir Christopher Wren, with all the other Renaissance Buildings, were held up to ridicule by a mistaken, but very enthusiastic band of young architects, who, with the best intentions of doing right, performed many most regrettable and destructive restorations. To-day one can scarcely realise what vandalism was perpetrated by these supposed purists. Men who were not architects are also responsible for desecration. I was recently told by the attendant of an important church in the North when I remarked on the peculiarity of some of the Norman Carvings, "They had been improved and finished by a local carver, but unfortunately they had not enough funds to finish them"; and another case from the South : a gentleman informed me he was on the City Council when the question was discussed of taking down a very fine mediaeval gateway to allow a circus procession to go through the town. The Council by one vote decided not to do so, but took down two old cottages at the side so that the procession could enter the city, and the beautiful gateway still remains.

WITHOUT THE WALLS.

Now let us imagine we have arrived at the railway station, and from the entrance we are able to see the old city, scattered over the opposite hillside, more closely built round the grand old church near the crown of the hill. We are particularly fortunate, for just now Nature is picture making, and through a break in a somewhat cloudy sky the sun streams down on the church and the surroundings, while the whole of the other parts are in shade. The south front is in strong light and the western side partly so ; had they been equally lighted it would have been 3 o'clock ; but it is not yet 2, and with a long afternoon before us we can leisurely walk down the hill, cross the stone bridge and mount the opposite hill by the winding road that opens to the Market Place from which a narrow cross street leads to the church. It is your first journey here, and you are interested in sketching Architecture. I have been here several times, and have made many sketches. I have brought a few with me to-day to show what I have done, and my method of doing it, so that in due time you may do as good or better work. Here is a sketch of the old farm-buildings we are approaching. You remark, " How very slight and yet how right it all seems," and you notice how sparing I have been with my ink, putting it mostly to represent the deeper shades and shadows and not putting a hard, black line round every part. Yes, I don't use so much ink ; I was early in life impressed with the fact that plenty of white paper is perhaps the most useful thing in a pen and ink sketch.

If we stand back from the field gate we have been looking over, I can give you the broad principles of light and shade, which will help you, to first look for, and then put into your sketches, the truths of tone. We are again fortunate, for the sun is now entirely hidden by the clouds, and a general grey light prevails,

under which condition it is best to first study tone. The strongest lights are on the top planes of all the objects—the top of the posts, the top of the top rail, of the lower rails, of the diagonal brace, the top of the strap hinges, of all fastenings, and on the ground itself, and the deep darks are on the underside, and all other parts receive their relative share of light and shade. If you once thoroughly realise the top light, underdark, and relative intermediate shades on all objects in grey light, you have the key to putting the "touches that tell" into a sketch.

In the farm building you see the underdarks at the eaves, under the shed roof, under the milkmaid, under her arms, under the branches of foliage that come forward ; and these most important depths of tone are carefully recorded in the sketch. Again I note a very good example of the little work needed for sufficient representation, in the wheels of the farm cart that is approaching us. See how as the tyre becomes more underside it also becomes darker, and how dark the undersides of the spokes as they get towards the horizontal position ; and these few truths of tone, if accurately represented, would sufficiently suggest the whole wheel.

As we walk down the hill you will notice how the horizon goes down with us. I have heard it remarked that there is a difficulty in representing down-hill, so I will explain how you may properly do so. On a straight stretch of railway, the rails seem to vanish up to a point *on* the observer's eye level—his or her horizon—in a similar way if the stretch is up-hill the lines seem to vanish up towards a point *above* the eye level of the observer, and on a stretch of down-hill the lines seem to vanish up towards a point *below* the eye level of the observer. If you will put your horizontal line high in your sketch, and let all lines on the down-inclined plane and all other lines actually parallel to them vanish upwards towards a point *below* your horizontal line—eye level—you will get a correct representation of down-hill. The lower you put this vanishing point the steeper will the hill be represented, and the effect is still further helped by a fence at the roadside, and figures on the road, with lines at their feet and their heads vanishing to the same point; but the eaves of a house and all other truly horizontal lines must of course vanish at a point *on* the horizontal line—eye level—a point directly in front of the observer and generally called the P.S.— point of sight.

Bridges vary in form according to locality. The one we are approaching I select from the North of Scotland, a picturesque old Gothic Bridge, built in 1320. A bridge of such a size could only have been

attempted on sound rock foundations, and contrasts with the low, sturdy bridges of many openings built on the softer subsoils in the flatter districts of the Midlands or South of England.

In my sketch of it, I ask you to notice particularly the underdarks, which are few but effective. We cross the bridge and approach a couple of simple cottages—brick-built and tiled—suggesting the South of England; and in my sketch you will see the up-hill suggested by the inclined line of road cutting the bottom

B

of the high wall and the house, and evidently vanishing at a higher point than the observer's eye level; the

sketch also shows that some few feet of the top of the road have been removed, to ease the incline of the hill, and this accounts for the unusual height of brickwork under the living-rooms, and the necessity for many steps to get to the entrance door and the garden behind.

Further up the hill we come to a group of stone-built houses covered with stone slates, suggesting

Derbyshire. The up-hill is not only shown in the sketch by the line of road at bottom of the buildings, but by the low level of the observer's horizon, and by

the higher position of the distant figure. On level ground the heads of all figures will be about one level, their feet getting higher as they are more distant. Going up-hill the heads of the figures will get higher as they are more distant (see sketch), and of course the feet higher too; going down-hill the heads of the figures will get lower as they are more distant, but the

feet must get *higher* though not much as the figures are more remote. A distant figure with the feet showing lower in the picture than the feet of a near figure on the same plane is an impossibility of representation.

We are just passing a modern cottage in the old Tudor, half timbered manner, called black and white in Lancashire and Cheshire. We will delay for a minute to note how well the old idea is carried out here; how the woodwork, not sawn square but adzed, is pinned together with wood pegs and oak wedges;

how the woodwork to posts and gate is again not sawn square but cleft and all so delightfully sketchable; again, note the simple and effective Italian form of chimney top, remedying the down draught that would have caused smoky chimneys and bad tempers. After making the sketch, I got to know the owner and designer of the cottage, and as you may imagine I found here an interesting personality—a friend and follower of Ruskin. This brings to my mind pleasant memories of the many charming people I have become acquainted with when out sketching.

The city we are visiting is an old Mediaeval one, but was a place of importance in Roman times, and the actual old Roman gate to the city is before us, still in use, a large archway over the road and a smaller one for pedestrians. It is a very fine bit of work, constructed with enormous stones nearly 2,000 years ago, and is a delightful subject for a sketch. You will see at once that a hard line would not at all represent these time worn stones; and one thinks of Ruskin's definition of a good line, the exact wording of which I don't at the moment remember, but the idea is : a line broken and irregular in length, being continuous in direction and having a vibratory life.

WITHIN THE WALLS.

Through the archway we are in the more important part of the city ; and the houses are somewhat plain, but very dignified, many of them having good bold Georgian cornices and especially good individual doorways. In domestic work equally with ecclesiastical, the entrance door has always received the greatest amount of elaboration and respect. In the latter the doorways are often the only part of the old church left to us. In the former, say in the Georgian Period, the windows were mere holes in the wall in comparison with the beautiful and proudful doorways ; and door respect is shown to-day, in the shining bell-pulls, knockers and whitened steps, and in some Northern districts the housewife of the smallest cottage with coloured stones puts a daily elaboration on her steps and every other bit of wrought stone-work at her door that she can reach ; and even where blocks of flats have been introduced, and their front doors have gone, they will open the bottom sash of their windows and colour the window sill and so much of the window dressings as is within reach. It is interesting to reflect for a moment that birds and all other animals, for obvious reasons, take every care to hide their nests ; and civilization tends, for less obvious reasons, to make us take every opportunity to proudly show ours. We stop for a moment to notice the doorway of Buckingham

House. The cornice is rather mongrel in form, but it has good, bold, carved trusses at the sides. The date is somewhere about 1700.

We next note a doorway with much more refined

AND HOW TO SKETCH IT.

detail, about 100 years later, in the Adam style. Robert and James Adam, two young Scotch architects, studied in Italy and brought some expert craftsmen home with them. They eventually got a very wide practice, and considerably influenced the Architecture of Great Britain, particularly in the elaborate but very refined plasterwork and interior fittings.

In this narrow street, close by, is one of the very earliest Nonconformist chapels; it has three very

interesting doorways, which much better illustrate good Renaissance work than the doorway of Buckingham House. The street widens and goes down-hill, and

we note an interesting covered market with rooms above. There is not much to indicate if the building is Tudor or early Jacobean; but time passes and we must now hurry on to the Church.

WITHOUT THE CHURCH.

This very interesting structure has the usual history. The old Saxon church, of which there are no remains except a small piece of rude walling seen in the crypt, was several times pillaged and burnt by the Danes, who often spent their summer holiday visiting the English churches. Then in Early Norman times a large church was begun, starting first to build the choir and transepts; for 100 years the work continued westwards. The Norman west front was pulled down by the succeeding Bishop and the nave lengthened by three bays—Transitional in style. At this date the style was changing so rapidly that the new west front had nothing in common with Norman Architecture, and remains one of the finest early illustrations of Early English or Gothic Architecture, built between 1200 and 1220. Part of the Norman Presbytery was then taken down, much enlarged, and built in the new manner. At three different periods the church was considerably damaged by fire. During the 14th century great building operations were going on. The Chapter House, much more decorated in manner, was finished in 1319. The rich woodwork of the stalls and Bishop's Throne, finished in 1324, are good examples of the Decorated or middle Gothic Period sometimes called Edwardian. Then the central Norman Tower fell, destroying part of the Nave, the remainder being found so damaged that it was decided to build a new Nave, the Archbishop granting forty days' indulgence to all who subscribed to the Building Fund. By this time the style was again changing, and the new Nave, completed in 1400, is one of the finest examples of Early Perpendicular work. The Tower was rebuilt about 100 years later, and is to-day considered one of our most beautiful Perpendicular Towers.

In the troubled later times this church suffered in common with the others, most of its get-at-able Art work being ruthlessly destroyed, and the horses of the Roundhead soldiers were stabled in the Nave.

I now give a list of the English Kings who reigned during the periods we are considering, and the usually accepted dates of the several Periods of Architecture.

Norman Period (124 years) see plate 5.
  William I   . 1066.
  William II   . 1087.
  Henry I   . 1100.
  Stephen   . 1135.
  Henry II   . 1154 to 1189 (Transition).
Early English Period (118 years) see plates 3 and 6.
  Richard I   . 1189 (Transition)
  John   . 1199.
  Henry III   . 1216.
  Edward I   . 1272 to 1307 (Transition).
Decorated Period (70 years) see plates 7 and 8.
  Edward II   . 1307.
  Edward III   . 1327 to 1377 (Transition at end of reign).

Perpendicular Period (170 years) see plates 2 and 4.
Richard II . 1377.
Henry IV . 1399.
Henry V . 1413.
Henry VI . 1422.
Edward IV . 1461.
Edward V . 1483.
Richard III . 1485.
Henry VII . 1485.
Henry VIII . 1509 to 1546.

PLATE I. FRONTISPIECE, CELTIC PRE-NORMAN. In the old burying ground round the church are several interesting tombstones of the last three centuries; some with dates about 1700 are more than usually good, and French in design, the style of Louis XIV, Louis XV. It is an unfortunate fact to record, but perfectly true, that our memorials to the dead are good as they are older, both as regards design and lettering. We have here one of the very oldest to see— one of the few remaining Celtic crosses of which we are justly proud. I have sketched nearly every one in the three countries and this is one of a very good type, and centuries older than any other part of the church. These crosses are mostly in Ireland.

We will now more particularly consider the characteristic forms of the different periods in detail, not taking them in actual sequence but dealing with that particular period that may be in view. In this case it happens to be Perpendicular, the nave and transept built about 1400, and the tower about the year 1500.

PLATE II. PERPENDICULAR PERIOD, 1377-1546. At first glance we notice the very large windows and the

AND HOW TO SKETCH IT.

PLATE II.

enormous buttresses between them, a very necessary matter when so little of the wall is left solid ; as well as to take the thrust of the heavy stone vaulting which covers the nave and aisles. The thrust is first taken by the flying buttress over the aisle roof and carried into the buttress on the outside of aisle walls, and is made much more effective by the heavy masses of stonework which form the pinnacles at the top. Pinnacles are just extra-weights designed for this very purpose, but at the same time forming decorative features of great value ; they were rarely used before the 14th century. These wide windows are the last form of Gothic Window Development. In Norman times the windows were single-light, narrow openings in very thick walls, with buttresses projecting only a few inches, the necessary abutment to the thrust from arch was sufficient in the thick walls ; each succeeding style has wider windows, thinner walls, and therefore deeper showing buttresses. Another characteristic of the perpendicular windows, beyond their greater size, is the perpendicular predominance in the form of the tracery and the horizontal bands called transoms, which cut across the mullions and divide the window into small panels. The same idea of panelling is often carried on the surface of the walls, becomes one of the characteristic elaborations of the period, and produces a very rich surface effect. You will also notice the main window arches are four-centred, not simple, two centred arches as mostly used in the Early English and Decorated Periods.

It may interest you to know that our English churches from east to west measure from 50 to 100 feet longer than any others in Europe, but the Continental examples are about half as wide again across the nave, about half as high again in internal height, and fully half as large again in area. So it will be seen that our great cathedral churches are much smaller than the continental ones, but at the same time we have a much longer vista from the western door looking east. Having seen the full flower, or as some will say the decaying flower, of late Gothic, we will now look at the bursting bud.

PLATE III. EARLY ENGLISH, 1189-1307. The very well known and justly admired west front, built about 1200, shows a remarkable advance on the round arched work of Norman times. It consists of three enormously wide, lofty and deeply recessed arches, the centre one being a little narrower; each arch capped with a gable richly arcaded, pierced by wheel windows and flanked by square towers again having their surfaces covered with ever varying arcades. The composition is a noble as well as a daring one, and entirely supersedes any other English example.

The central porch was built in the latter part of the next century, probably to strengthen the construction, and is really a very beautiful example of transition from the Decorated to the Perpendicular Periods. The window on the inner wall under the nearest main arch has both vertical and horizontal lines in the tracery, so of course is a window inserted in the Perpendicular Period. Vertical mullions were used in the two previous styles, but in the Perpendicular Period these mullions are often continued up through the tracery to the main arch instead of merging into the carved tracery itself.

Plate III.

Before entering the church you will notice on the oak door a grotesque head formed in metal, with a heavy ring in its mouth for a knocker ; this was used in the olden times by criminals and others who sought sanctuary. Two attendants alternately slept and watched that no applicant knocked in vain ; a truly christian institution of the 12th century, now out of date, at least in England.

WITHIN THE CHURCH.

PLATE IV. PERPENDICULAR, 1377-1546. Now within the church, after a few minutes' awed and silent contemplation, we step aside into the north aisle, and looking diagonally, can better see the lofty four-centred arcade arches with panelled surface between them and the clerestory windows. We see the large perpendicular window in the opposite aisle, and note the distinctly perpendicular octagonal capitals and bases of the arcade piers, and that the sections of the mouldings have the hollows more pronounced than the rounded parts ; we further note that several of the members of the pier mouldings run right up and round the arches without being stopped by intervening capital ; we further note the plan of pier is greater from N. to S. than from E. to W. ; these are all indications of the Perpendicular Period. The full forms of the 14th-century mouldings always seem to me so typical of the fullness of life ; and the hollows, which get more used and pronounced as this period continues, seem so typical of decline. There are no hollows in fine form ; the seeming hollows of perfect humanity will be found to be a series of smaller fulnesses. This will show what

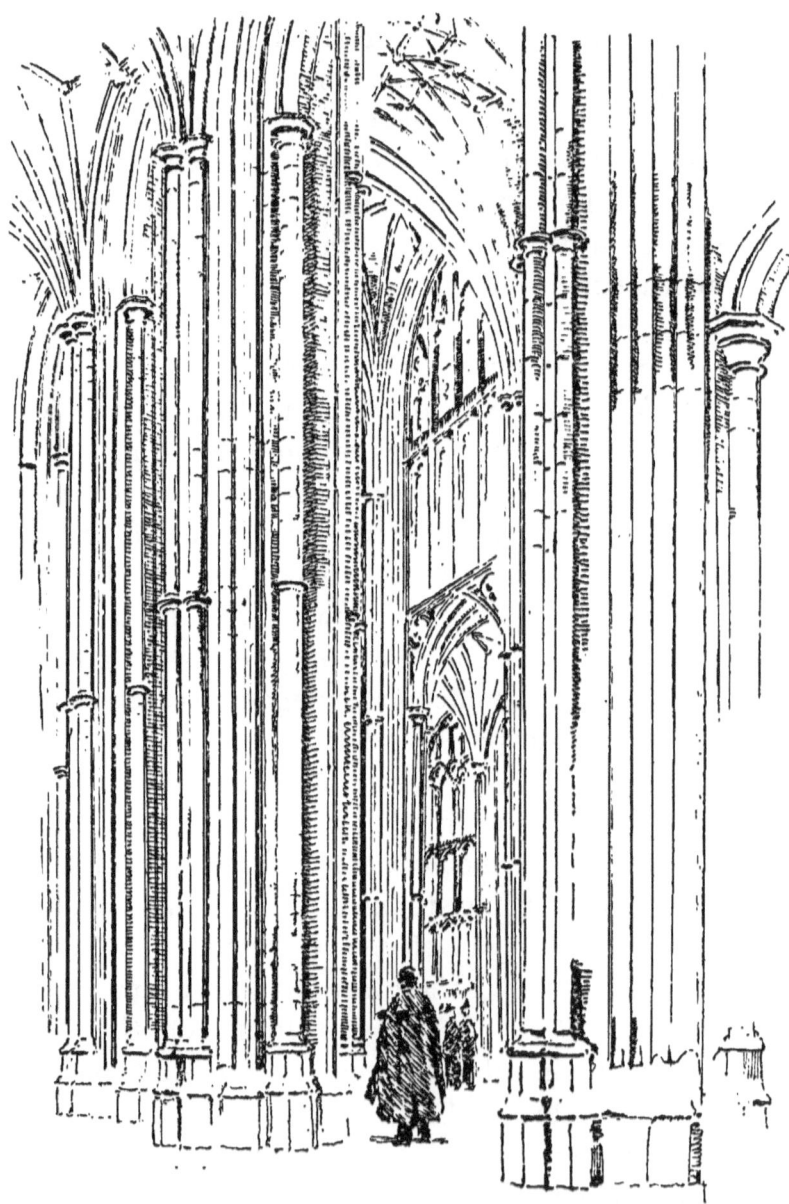

PLATE IV.

is meant and felt by those who remark, "His drawing is so full"; of another, "His drawing is poor and thin." Square formed pateras and crockets with angular detail are characteristic ornaments, and a free use of the Tudor rose ; the detail generally becoming less beautiful as the style becomes older in years.

Crossing to the south aisle we find a Norman Font (NORMAN, 1066-1189) of pleasing form, enriched with rude carvings now too dilapidated to be clearly understood. The succeeding church builders seem to have respected both the old Norman doorways and the fonts; and in several churches, where every other detail of the Norman Period is destroyed, we

yet find a Norman doorway in a very good state of preservation. In the case of the fonts it may be their massiveness, or even their usefulness for other purposes will have preserved them from destruction : many of them after Reformation times were used in the neighbouring farms as drinking troughs for horses or cattle. Be the cause what it may, the

C

fact remains there are a large number of Norman doorways and Norman fonts still in existence.

The date of this example is probably right at the end of the Period.

PLATE V. NORMAN; ROMANESQUE; ROUND ARCHED; 1066-1189. Walking up the nave and under the central tower we come to the Norman work in the Presbytery, an arcade of semicircular arches with wide dividing piers : slightly projecting from the face of the wall is a pilaster with roll moulding at the angles. The arches of the arcade are recessed several times ; the angles having a roll on some planes and being square edged at others ; the outer plane is enriched with the chevron—or Zigzag—the most characteristic Norman ornament ; projecting string courses with axed ornament on face run horizontally over the arches. Above the arcade is the Triforium or Blind story as it is sometimes called ; in this particular case it is open on each side ; in its more usual form it is placed over the vaulting of the aisle and under the aisle roof, and forms a passage round the church at this level. Above this triforium is an Early English clerestory having high windows to light the nave. In Norman, Early English and Decorated churches of any importance we generally find the arcade, triforium and clerestory, but in the Perpendicular Period the triforium is more frequently entirely missing or has become a series of vertical panels as we saw in the nave. Between the main arch and the two smaller ones of the triforium, the recessed surface is covered with bands of axed decoration.

There is an interesting detail at the top of the Norman

PLATE V.

Pilaster. The Early English designer found a wide projecting mass of stone which he did not want, so he placed two small crocketted gables on it and between them started the delicate trefoil shaft to carry his vaulting ribs. This illustration well shows the wonderful change of style from the Massive Norman to the graceful Early English which closely followed it.

The characteristic ornaments used in this Period are round or square alternate billets, the chevron or Zigzag, cable, saw tooth, pellet or stud, fret, various interlacings, a continuation of the old Celtic ornament (see Frontispiece), the bead and roll, bird's beak and cat-head, leaf scroll, roses, mythological animals, signs of the Zodiac and rude illustrations of the common incidents of life. There is a well-known quaint series representing the birth of a child, several further incidents in his life till he gets married; the story now ends with a representation of him and his wife in the same boat, but alas! they are pulling in opposite directions.

There is a charming individuality introduced in the simple elements of Norman and Early Gothic ornaments by their arrangement. The arch stones were all sorts of widths: 4 in., 5 in., 6 in., or any other largest possible stone they could cut out of the block; they then arranged, say, the zigzag so that there should be one, two or three on each stone: the result is, some of the zigzags looked at individually seem cramped, others seem over wide; but seen as a whole they as thoroughly satisfy the mind of an artist as they dissatisfy the modern mechanic. The so-called Gothic restorers entirely missed this spirit of individuality in the old work and restored with a mechanical cast-iron-like regularity that is particularly offensive to lovers of the old work and students of nature.

PLATE VI. EARLY ENGLISH, 1189-1307. Crossing to the South Transept we see some very noble Early English work. The windows of this first Gothic period are single lights with arches generally formed on the equilateral triangle, they are often arranged in twos, threes, fives, etc., and are in different heights so that they compose under a single arch ; the mouldings are rounds and hollows, the rounds varied with one, two or more fillets : the general effect is rather pipe-like. The plans of pier are very various, a common one being a large central circular or octagonal shaft surrounded by small circular ones, which are sometimes detached and often of Purbeck marble.

The abacus—top of capital—is round on plan, the old square and chamfer section of the Norman has become two rolls with a deep hollow between. The capitals are very various in design : the finest are beautifully carved with conventional forms that sometimes approach the Greek treatment of the bud of the honeysuckle ; the general carving is so distinct in effect from that of any other Gothic period that it soon becomes strongly impressed on the memory and most easily recognised. Bands, similar to the abacus, cut the long shafts into shorter heights, the bands being sometimes stone, sometimes marble, and again sometimes metal. The bases are formed of rolls with fillets and intermediate hollows ; arcades are used on the walls with varying formed arches: sharp pointed, flat pointed, circular, trefoil, and pointed trefoil as in this example. The whole style is particularly refined and pure. The most common

38 ARCHITECTURE

PLATE VI.

ornament is the dog-tooth ; in a single Galilee porch there are more than 5,000 of these pyramid forms. The crocket, a rolled-up ornament resembling a young fern-frond or a reminiscence of the volute of the Corinthian Capital, is constantly used on the angles of spires and canopies, and often in piers and arches in the hollows between the rolls.

About 1280 there was a distinct change of form in the carving now all naturalistic in design and particularly delicate in execution. There is a certain chapter-house in the Midlands full of this wonderful carving, so deftly executed that it well repays for a long journey to see it ; it is finished as carefully at the back as on the front, which has probably created the saying, " It was done for the gods who do not judge from the outside." Through the Decorated period, the hollow bell of the capital is still retained, but the foliage rounds out into a full form rather encircling than growing out as in the earlier examples ; in the following Perpendicular period the carving goes, the bell reappears, the abacus being generally octagonal and hard in form.

I have only space to just touch the great subject of Gothic Architecture (and very few examples can be possible in so small a book). But before leaving the beautiful Early English period, here is a hint for those who find a difficulty in remembering dates : 1234 cannot easily be forgotten ; it is a date when many of the most beautiful examples were being constructed.

PLATE VII. DECORATED PERIOD, 1307-1377. In the Chapter-house we have an eight-sided chamber of great richness and a good example of the earlier

40 ARCHITECTURE

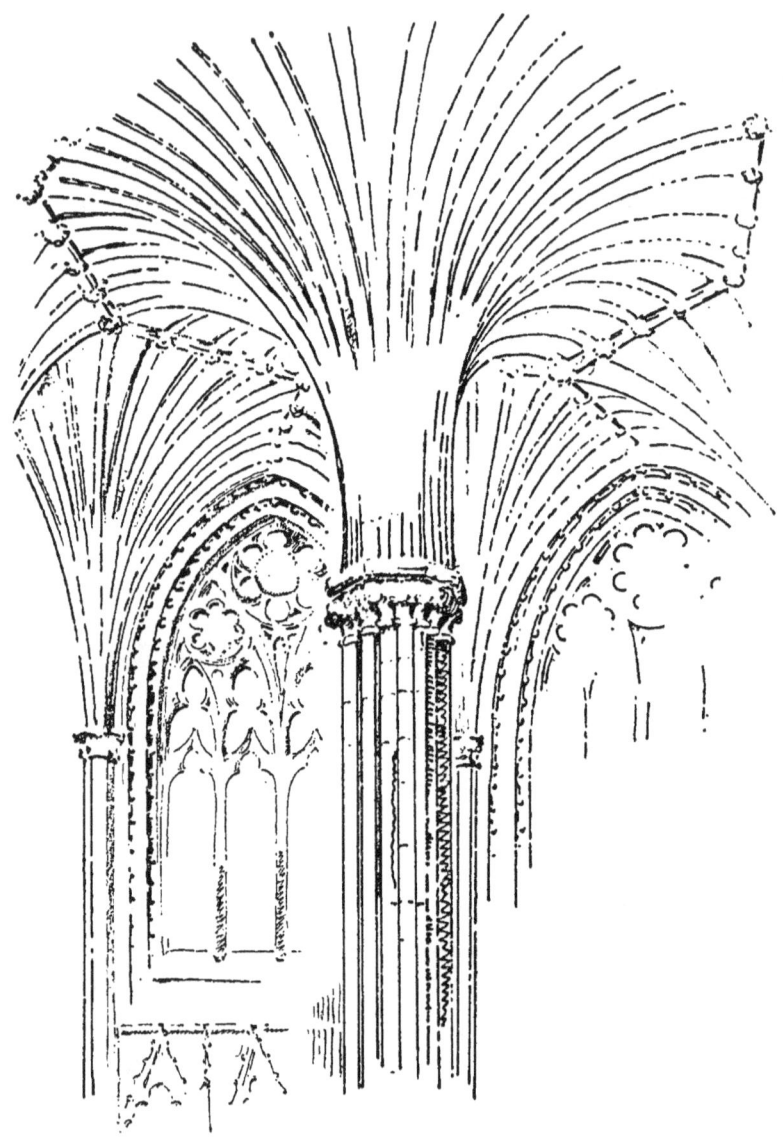

PLATE VII.

Decorated Period. The progress of window development between the grouped single lights of the Early English and the still more elaborate and larger windows of the Perpendicular Period is well shown here. The characteristic ornament of this earlier Decorated period is the ball flower, rows of which are seen in the hollows to jamb and arch of the windows; it is a sort of bud of three or four petals just open enough to show a ball inside. The carving of the earlier work was quite naturalistic as already described, but a beautiful conventionality was introduced into the best work of later times of the period. The theme was taken from some natural plant, then the leaves and flowers were carved with rounds and hollows on the main rib and a similar treatment on the side ribs. The variety of sizes of these rounds produced the very finest decorative work that we have ever created in England; and of which we may be justly proud. I am quite anxious to tell you where to go for the finest examples of Great Britain, but this book is not in competition with either histories of Architecture or guides to individual examples, so I will say instead. learn to recognise this style; find your own examples, they are fairly common—you will probably find some in the first church you examine.

My space is so limited, and my subject is so vast, that I can only just touch perhaps the greatest glory and certainly the highest scientific attainment of the Gothic Builders; of course, I mean the vaulted ceilings. The illustration here is a specimen of vaulting intermediate between the ruder Norman vaults and the extremely elaborate later Tudor work. I cannot

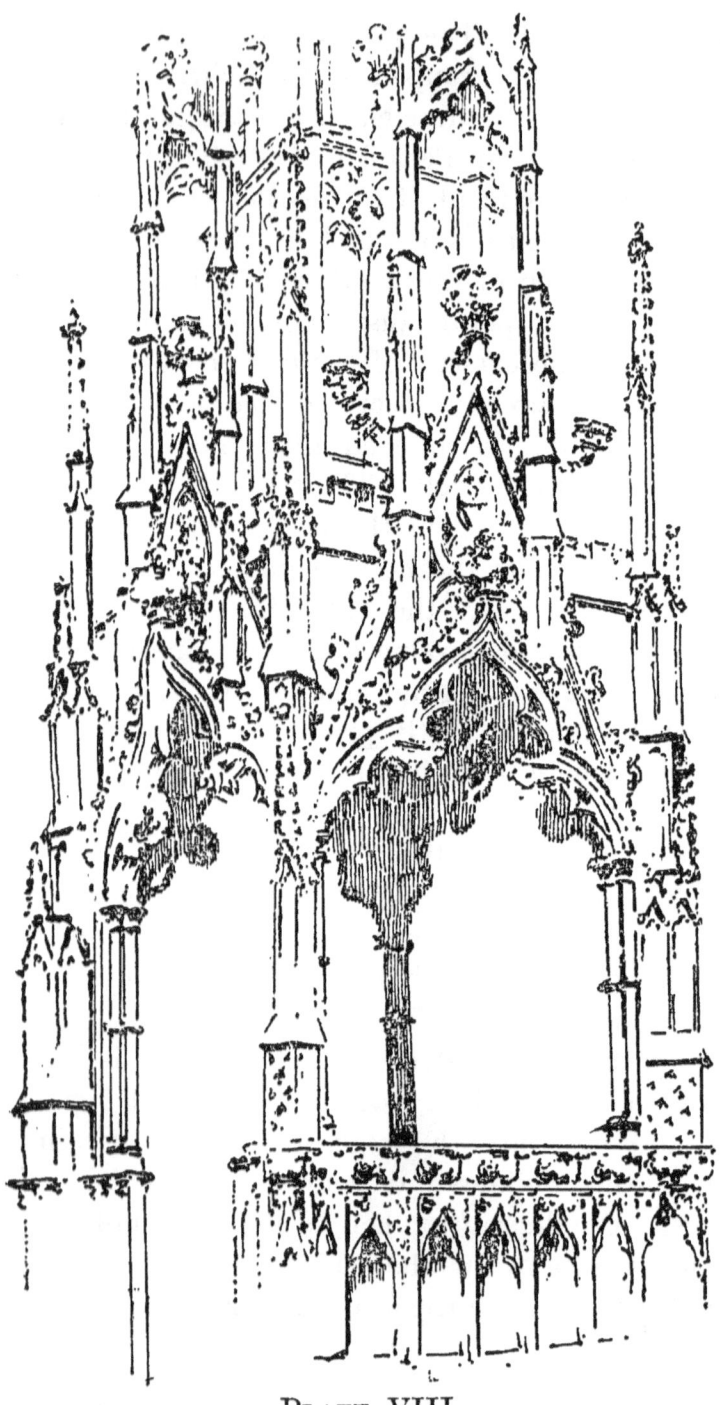

Plate VIII.

even touch the great subjects of Timber roofs or Sculpture at all.

PLATE VIII. DECORATED PERIOD, 1307-1377. For another example of this beautiful style we cannot do better than look at the fine woodwork of the choir stalls; more particularly the Bishop's throne; it is a little later in the period than the last example; at once we note the large arches turn a little outwards towards the apex; this ogee arch, sometimes very narrow, very wide, or intermediate as shown here, is a great indication of this date; the form is much more used in the decorative features than in the arcade or other constructional arches. This throne is so beautiful in design, and so honest in workmanship, that words will scarcely describe it. A curious little bit of information is that it cost £12. The oak was £4 and the labour £8—how values have changed since then.

I think I have finished my duties as showman of the church, but have yet to briefly explain some of the simple truths of representation so that you who have seen a little of my work may go and do your share in recording those things that more particularly appeal to you.

HOW TO SKETCH ARCHITECTURE.

Rapid and Accurate Representation.

REPRESENTATION of any object should not only be correct according to its perspective, but should also be pleasing to the eye; which only sees a limited portion at one time and not the whole subject in front of observer—as so many people try to sketch—and which the wide angle lense of the camera takes in, with all the ugly distortion of objects towards the edges of the photograph; so you see it is necessary to find the proper distance away; which is the right position for the sketcher to stand when he makes a sketch. Different individuals will have slightly different angles of vision, but it is generally agreed by experienced sketchers that the usually taught angle of 60° is too great for a pleasant sketch. I adopted, and for several years have used, in a series of more than 1000 Architectural Sketches, a very simple rule.

Step, or otherwise measure, or even estimate the length of the longest side of a building and stand at least that distance away from the nearest corner; or, if the object is high rather than wide, such as a church tower, measure or estimate the greater height or depth of the object above or below the eye level, and stand at least three times that height or depth away from nearest corner of the object. As an illustration, to sketch a man 6 ft. high I would stand at least 6 yards away. To sketch a tower 100 ft. high I would stand at least 100 yards away. To sketch an angle view of a building having the longest side 100 ft. long I would stand at least 100 ft. away.

To sketch an object of 5 ft. above or below eye level I would stand at least 5 yards away. By horizontally holding up to your eye a 2 ft. rule, with one of the divisions turned up at right angles, as shown in the illustration, you are at the proper distance to sketch all that is between the eye level and the top point of rule; and if you will then revolve the rule right round it will show you how much of the object or view in front of you can properly be sketched. I have drawn a white dotted line on the photograph to more clearly show this. If some part of the tower or object is higher than would be within the dotted line you must walk further away. I often use this

method of measuring a high building. When I have got to a point from which the top of building cuts to the top of the turned-up arm of rule when held horizontally, I note the exact point on the ground where I am standing, and strike from it to the tower; my stride being one yard, I know that if I make 100 strides, then the tower is 100 ft. high, or more exactly, 100 ft. above eye level.

Having settled my position as to distance, I decide

on the particular view I wish to sketch, and as the subject may happen to be mostly above or mostly below the eye level, I place my horizontal line low or high as the case may require. This horizontal line represents my horizon or eye level, and is the most important line to help truthful representation, for all forms are modified as they are near or remote from this line, which is always truly horizontal, and contains most of the vanishing points for other lines in the sketch. I now decide on some particular point on the eye level, which I look at when sketching, and this point, called the point of sight, is again a very important one. We will take it at the nearest corner of the building, and draw a slight vertical line to represent the corner on the sketch. I strongly advise that in all early sketches these two lines, one to represent the sketcher's eye level and the other vertically through the point of sight, shall be clearly defined. The ephemeral newspaper illustrations can be made very instructive if one gets into the way of deciding the position of, and drawing these two lines on the pictures. The eye of sketcher or lens of camera will have always been directly in front of the crossing of these two lines.

A good photograph shows every part of the view in true relation to the camera lens level, and the camera lens position; in other words, all is in true perspective.

A satisfactory sketch should have every part relative to the sketcher's eye level, and to a point on that eye level immediately opposite his eye; and should not be a series of sketches, of parts of the view, got by directing the eye to these parts in turn.

Without proper perspective this last untruthful sketch is almost inevitable; and through imperfect teaching, often by people who do not sketch themselves, any number of sketches are made on this untruthful eye-wandering basis.

A reliance on eye training—which is generally very slight—is often misleading; *measurement is the basis of accuracy.* Instead of holding a pencil at arm's length to get measurement of height or width, I deal with the matter in one operation, and hold a transparent celluloid set square as shown in photograph —a 60° 30° is the best form—at any distance in front

of my eye. Sliding my thumbs along the edge and keeping the thumb of my left hand at my eye level I at once get accurate proportions, say height and width of a church. These proportions I now transfer on to my sketch, and they—height above my horizon— and width—become standards of measurement, to which all other dimensions of the view and sketch must be relative. I can alter the scale of sketch larger or smaller by holding the celluloid set square further from or nearer to my eye.

A measuring set square with a scale on two edges is made by Messrs. Rowney. It has the sharp angles rounded off, so is nicer to handle and carry in pocket or sketch book.

A Simple Building.

If you stand in front of any building, looking diagonally towards the nearest corner, and hold out one arm at eye level parallel to the front, and the other arm at eye level parallel to the side, your extended fingers will point to the vanishing points of the sides to which the arms are parallel ; these vanishing points will be on your eye level, and in the sketch on the horizontal line, extended beyond the limits of picture. Such a view is sometimes called angular perspective to distinguish it from such a view as Fig. 1, Plate IX, where the vanishing point of ends come within the picture and the front does not vanish at all, it being a parallel perspective view.

PLATE IX. If we stand in front of a building, at sufficient distance away to properly see it, the horizontal lines of front will remain horizontal, the horizontal lines of ends will vanish towards their vanishing point—in this case the point of sight immediately in front of sketcher, Fig. 1. The front remains as a geometrical drawing, except the sides of roof that converge towards a point immediately over the vanishing point of the horizontals of end of house.

If the front is slightly inclined from sketcher, it will lose width ; and all its details, such as doors, windows,

AND HOW TO SKETCH IT. 49

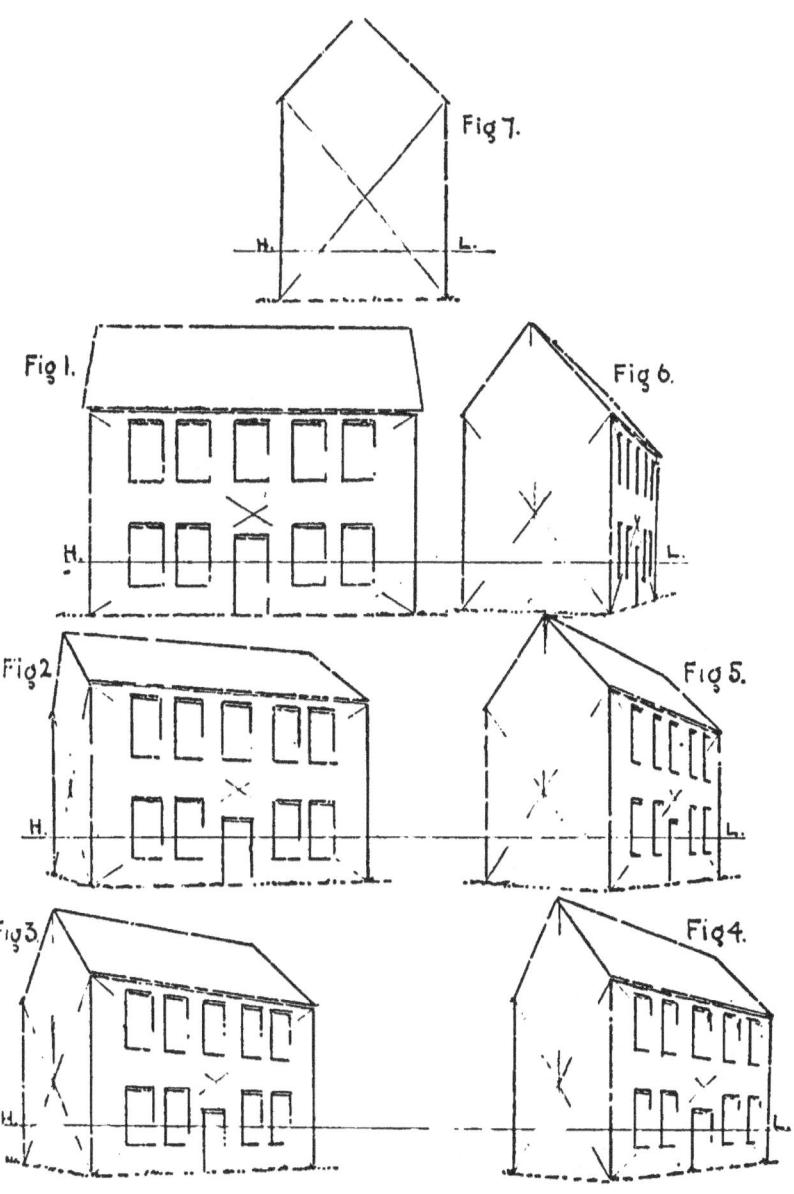

PLATE IX.

D

etc., will also lose width, and all the horizontal lines on the front will incline to a very distant V.P. This V.P.—Vanishing Point—is in each case on the eye level, and as the front is more inclined away, it and all its details lose more width, and the horizontal lines go to a nearer V.P. The front of Fig. 2 inclines 15°; of Fig. 3, 30°; of Fig. 4, 45°; of Fig. 5, 60°; of Fig. 6, 75°; in Fig. 7 the front is at 90° and not visible, the view is one in parallel perspective similar to Fig. 1.

A very careful examination and re-examination of this plate will make evident some simple but very important truths of representation, that occur, or should occur, in all Architectural Sketches. The main truths are :—

(1) *All receding lines actually parallel to each other incline towards their common V.P.*

(2) *If these lines are actually horizontal the V.P. is on the eye level—sketcher's horizon.*

(3) *Doors, windows and other features get narrower as they get remote from the near corner—further within the picture.*

(4) *Lines drawn from the opposite corners of the front or side will cross at the perspective centre, and give the true position for all parts exactly central—as the apex of gable at side of house—or centre of entrance door on front.*

(5) *The sloping sides of the ends of roof being parallel to each other will vanish at a V.P. in a vertical line through the V.P. of side of house; the near up-hill ends vanish upwards; the distant down-hill ends vanish downwards.*

(6) *As these gable slopes are equal—of the same inclination—their V.P.'s will be at equal distances above and below the eye level.*

OUTSIDE OF A CHURCH.

In this illustration the lines marked a., being parallel to each other, and also being horizontal and on a plane inclining away, will therefore recede towards a V.P. on the eye level, and the lines marked b. will recede towards a V.P. on the eye level on the other side.

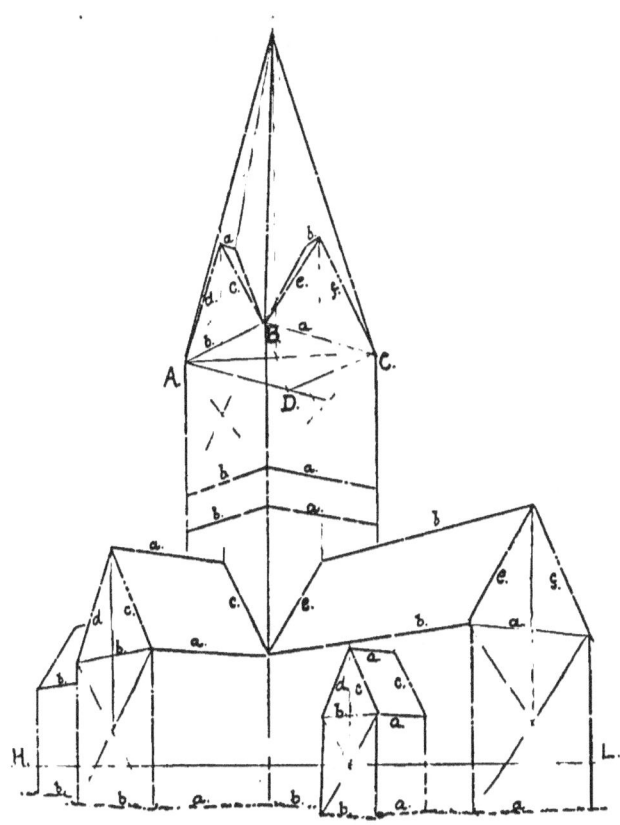

The nearer up-hill sloping lines c.c.c. are parallel to each other and vanish upwards towards a point in vertical line through the V.P. of the plane on which they are placed. The more distant down-hill sloping lines d.d.d. vanish downwards to a correspondingly placed V.P. In a similar way the nearer up-hill lines e.e.e. and the distant down-hill lines f.f. vanish upwards and downwards respectively.

Inside of a Church.

Interior views are often considered more difficult; but as the point of sight is also the V.P. and is always within the sketch, they are really less difficult, especially if one is satisfied to only draw so much of the view as can actually be seen.

The essential in a sketch such as shown in illustration

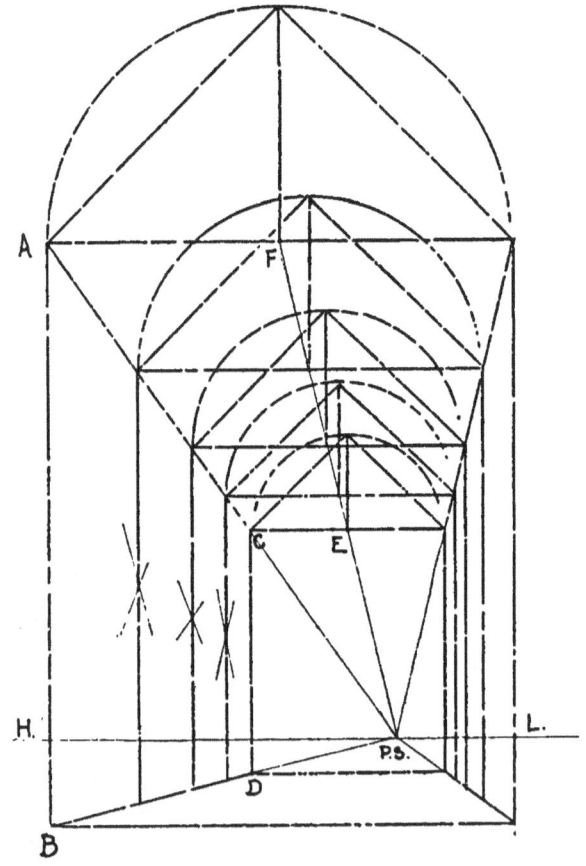

AND HOW TO SKETCH IT. 53

is the absolutely correct representation of A.B.C.D. relative to the eye level, and to the position of the sketcher and the width relative to the height. The line E.F. through the centre of width will enable one to correctly draw the roof timbers ; points for groining ; centres for semicircular arches, or whatever detail obtains. The figure A.B.C.D. can be divided up as required by diagonals, and from the points found on this side horizontal lines will give the corresponding points on the opposite side. This is a sketch in Parallel Perspective, one side—in this case the end being parallel to the picture plane—or imaginary large sheet of glass or picture plane through which we see the view. A sketch itself is a small scale representation of the picture plane.

Octagonal Forms.

In font, pulpit, tower, etc., we find numerous examples of the use of the Octagon in Architectural

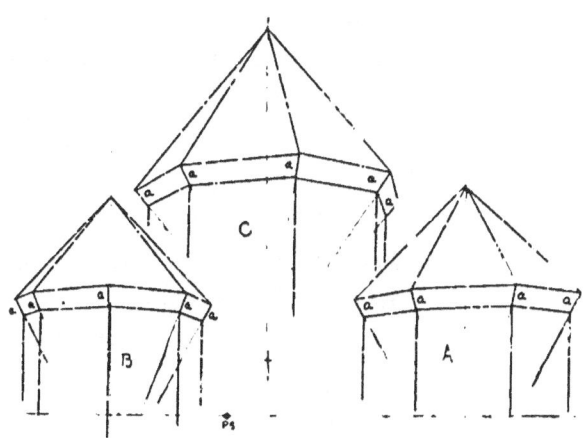

Design, and it is one of the acknowledged difficult forms to draw; presenting as it does very varying form in its several positions. In illustration I purposely show two very ugly positions of this figure : A the commonplace almost geometrical view ; B the straight joint running vertically through view. As both these are ugly, we may logically expect a pleasant view in the intermediate position ; and at C I show a view that is entirely satisfactory ; for the sides are all unequal in width, the angles of receding planes are all different, and we have a representation full of variety, hence beauty ; all the slope lines of roof are at different angles but meet at a point in a vertical line through centre of octagon on plan ; and all the sloping mitre lines at a.a.a. will meet at a point in this same vertical centre line.

Sketchers of Architectural forms will find these hints of use ; they are the outcome of using a method that gives perspective truths as surely as the accuracy of geometrical representation. A reliance on eye-training allows a sketcher to constantly miss these and many other details of accurate representation.

ARCHES.

The correct drawing of arches, as of circles, is generally again a difficulty to the unaided sketcher. One is very much helped as soon as he understands the correct representation of circles in every position of the picture. The illustration shows circles correctly drawn in containing squares, continued over all parts of the picture plane, in order to better show how the ellipses are modified in shape and inclination of axes, as they are placed relatively to the eye level and nearness to vertical line through the point of sight.

A careful study of this plate will show that the ellipses representing the circles have the long axes vertical; only when they are at the eye level, the axes

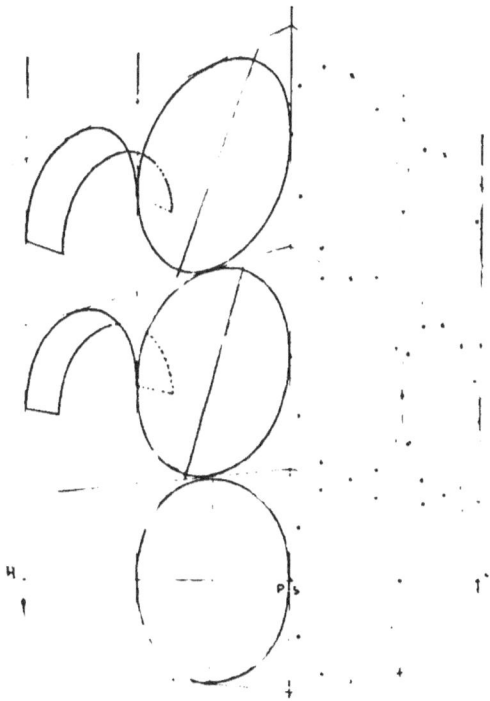

are tilted on the next row, and more tilted still on the top row.

Gothic pointed arches are just parts of circular arches with the top part omitted and the sides brought closer together. I advise that this plate be studied and re-studied until these truths of accurate representation are thoroughly understood.

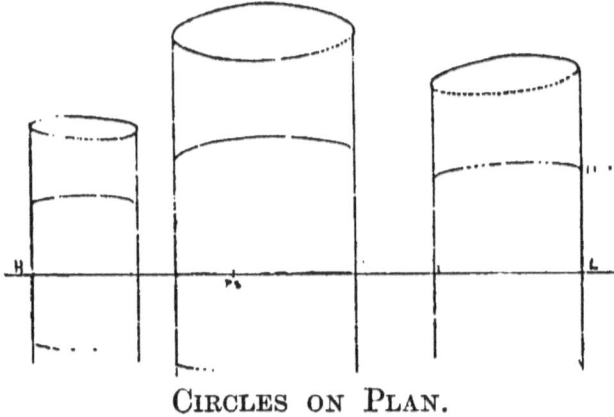

CIRCLES ON PLAN.

The above illustrates the accurate representation of circles on plan; seen in joints to large Norman piers, Early English capitals, bands and bases, fonts and other details.

On the nearer column the long axes of the ellipses are nearly horizontal because of their position on the vertical line through point of sight. On the column to the left the axis of top ellipses slightly inclines downwards, and at a joint the same distance below the eye level it would incline upwards to the same extent; at twice the height above eye level the axis would incline twice as much; at half the height it would incline half as much. The axis of the top ellipse to the right inclines much more because it is further away from vertical through point of sight.

Another important point is the openness of the ellipses accordingly as they are near or remote from the eye level. In sketching all such details I first sketch to the best of my ability one of these forms remote from the eye level and then logically draw in others with relative openness of form, using mind-inference rather than eye-judgment, and in all cases drawing the complete form of ellipse.

Mr. Roberts' Architectural sketches are made on a slightly transparent paper over the perspectively ruled squared paper of R.'s method of Perspective, which enables him to draw directly the finished sketch in ink.

Bank note paper pocket sketch books 7 in. by 4 in. with 7 diagrams of R.'s Method of Perspective and instructions, 5s.

The above sizes are stocked by George Rowney & Co.

Special measuring celluloid set squares made to Mr. R.'s specification, price 2/6 each.

www.ingramcontent.com/pod-product-compliance
Lightning Source LLC
Chambersburg PA
CBHW022336230426
43664CB00040B/1276